time to dance

the integration of movement in the primary curriculum

Written by Marion Ware
Illustrated by Lyn Gray

First published in 1987 by
Belair Publications Ltd.,
P.O. Box 12, Twickenham, England, TW1 2QL
© Marion Ware, 1987.
Cover design by Laurence Dunmore
Design, setting and artwork by Solo Graphics
ISBN 0 947882 06 5

The Author and Publishers
would like to thank
children and staff in the
London Boroughs of Enfield, Hounslow
and Richmond-upon-Thames

Printed and Bound in Hong Kong by World Print Ltd

contents

introduction

This book is a collection of primary classroom topics, each presenting ideas across the curriculum, but with the emphasis in each case being upon Dance. Each dance has developed from my work as a Junior class teacher, but I have also used them in Infant and Special schools in my role as a Dance Support teacher.

Some of the dances were designed to initiate a topic, some were a by-product of children's interests, and other lessons were developed to link the classroom work with their physical education programme. I see the 'Hall' period as an extension of the classroom, and find that there are endless opportunities to integrate Physical Education (in this instance Dance) with other aspects of the curriculum. In particular, some of the best creative written work has been produced after a dance lesson.

'The Sea'

Curving, curling, it silently twirls.
It ripples and swirls,
Getting bigger as it goes.
Making crashing waves that spiral along.

Underneath the surface
The seaweed is swishing
Making patterns as it flows
With the current,
Then becoming calm
Silent
And still.

Written by a 2nd year Junior class after a dance lesson.

Whenever I feel the need to explain to children the feeling of movement required, I use analogies just as I would do in any other part of the curriculum. Because the children feel the movement, however, the vocabulary seems to be learnt more efficiently.

Each dance in this book can be seen as a recipe. The first time of using each, there may be a need to follow the ideas methodically, but in subsequent lessons, because they have become part of your repertoire, the ideas are easily adaptable to suit your own approach. Obviously your way of presenting each dance may vary depending on the age of the children you teach.

The music on the 'Time to Dance' tape was written specifically for the 15 dances in this book. The three parts of each dance are introduced separately and then the three are repeated without a break in between. In this way you can take the children through each dance in its individual sections, and repeat the whole without having to rewind the tape.

At the end of the book under 'Variations on the Dances' I have listed themes or dramatic approaches which could be used with the same basic movements and the musical accompaniment on the tape. The 15 pieces of music are obviously usable in many ways, and I am sure you will find that they inspire you to experiment with other movement sessions with completely different themes to the ones I have suggested.

Each dance recipe has been made from the following basic ingredients:

1. 5 basic types of movement: travel, turn, jump, gesture and pause.
2. Body parts: head, fingers, hands, wrists, elbows, arms, bottom, legs, knees and toes.
3. A quality of movement: speed – medium or slow
   effort – strong or light
   flow – simultaneous or in succession
   shape – round, long, twisted
4. Where in space: Direction – forwards, backwards, upwards, downwards.
   Levels – high, low.
5. Relationships: with whom they are dancing: self, teacher, partner, group, object.
6. Accompaniment: percussion, music, sound.

It is important that as teachers of a physical skill, we pay as much attention to the details of planning and organisation in the hall as we would in the classroom. Here are a few ideas:-

- Compile a collection of your favourite music, videos and pictures.
- Familiarise yourself with a variety of musical instruments.
- Have available good audio equipment (especially with A.P.P.S. facility).
- Give instructions clearly and, where necessary, with the use of analogies.
- Use your voice to fit the movement.
- Never be afraid of repetition.
- Insist on a starting and finishing position.
- Be prepared to be a director, sculptor and designer of children's work. They can only learn the skill of stagecraft from what they see.
- Always provide a warm-up.
- Within each lesson try to provide a contrast of movement: where a child bends, he then stretches.

If we are to recognise and respond to today's multicultural society, we cannot ignore the wealth of dances implicit in every culture. The steps, rhythm and formation can be used to enrich the children's creative work.

Dance is a performance art. If you have the confidence to teach it, go on to present it as a performance. The children will respond. Dance needs to be seen: it is as much for the audience as the dancers.

I am in agreement with the H.M.I. report which discusses dance under the heading of 'Aesthetic and Creative', and suggests that dance develops the physical, emotional and cognitive as well as the social elements of developmental growth. I believe that Dance is an underused resource, and that many teachers see it purely as a subject and not as a teaching method. It is both.

Whatever happens, enjoy yourself, enjoy the children, and they will benefit in many ways.

Marion Ware

balloons

Balloons, Part 2 (arranged for a special assembly): The balloons bob backwards and forwards, with the strings held by a balloon-seller.

STIMULUS: *Selection of balloons, inflated and deflated, of different shapes and colours, attached and free-floating.*
OR a picture of a balloon seller.

DISCUSSION AND OBSERVATION: Allow children to observe a balloon being blown up, and released, and listen to the sound. Provide children with the opportunity to play with balloons to experiment in a free situation; inflating, deflating, slowly/quickly, popping with a pin. Take a balloon for a walk inside and outside.

LANGUAGE: Creative writing:
- "Escape by hot-air balloon"
- "The balloon's journey".

Punctuation: speech balloons and speech marks.

Vocabulary: list words associated with ballooning and hot air ballooning. Develop into poetry.

Balloon debate: Situation given – the children are all riding in a hot-air balloon which is sinking dangerously. To gain height one person must be thrown out. Children give reasoned arguments as to why they should remain. They may act as historical characters or famous people of today.

SCIENCE: Air pressure, currents.
Heat: hot-air balloons/Helium balloons.
Weather, and weather balloons in forecasting.
Elasticity: related experiments.

HISTORY: Early flight
The Hindenberg Disaster
Natural flight evolution

POEMS: 'The Balloon' (an extract) Oscar Wilde, from *Fancy Free*, Poems selected by D. Saunders, Evans Bros. Ltd.
'Spells: to be said to a balloon being blown up' from *I'll tell you a Tale*, Ian Serraillier, Puffin Books.
'The Balloon Man', E. Herbert, in *The Book of a Thousand Poems*.

BOOKS: *Papa, Please Get the Moon for me*, Eric Carle, Hodder & Stoughton
The Red Balloon, Albert Lamorise, Unwin.
Winnie the Pooh, A. A. Milne, Methuen.
Around the World in Eighty Days, Jules Verne, Jonathan Cape.
Things that Go, Usborne Publishing Ltd., 1981.

MUSIC: 'Balloons', Moriel Gidney, *Time to Dance* tape, Belair Publications Ltd.
Percussion: Fill balloons with various mediums, e.g. rice, water.
Experiment by shaking, releasing air and holding neck.

ART/CRAFT: Collage of balloons, painted, printed or drawn.
Design and make a hot-air balloon.
Exploding pictures: cut out a picture (face or words) from a magazine. Cut into equal strips, either horizontal or vertical. Mount picture on plain background leaving a parallel space between each strip. The gaps can vary in depth, starting close but getting bigger.
Expanding faces – draw onto a balloon. Blow up and draw the faces at various stages – leads to enlarging and co-ordinate work.
Class mural – each child paints a self portrait. The pictures are cut out and mounted on a background, together with real balloons on string, attached to the backing with double-sided tape. (See illustration)

WARM-UP: Let's play hopscotch. Roll the stone, pretend to jump into the first two squares, landing on two feet. Now jump onto one foot. Hopscotch in every direction. Don't go in a circle. Make sure you're bending your knees. Stop. Gently bend your knees and stretch up on to your toes. Stretch all the way through your body to the tips of your fingers. Hopscotch again. Off you go. Stop. Can you try to jump from two feet onto two feet? From two feet on to one foot? From one foot on to one foot, and from one foot back to two feet. Practise that again. Can you do your pattern backwards? Careful, don't fall over.

---------------- • ----------------

INFLATION: Watch me as I blow into this balloon. It's getting bigger and bigger, but it started crumpled and creased. Find a position on the floor and make your body crumpled and creased.
I'm going to blow you up, and as you swell, what shapes can you make? They must be rounded shapes and strong. You're pushing out the elastic skin of the balloon. Stop.
Notice how the balloon shrinks slightly as I pause to take a breath. Let me inflate you again, but when I take a breath, can you shrink slightly too?
Swell again. You're getting bigger and bigger, and hold .. now relax. Try this with the music **(BALLOONS, PART 1)**.

LOOK FOR:
– OPPORTUNITIES TO ENCOURAGE GOOD SHAPE.
– USE OF GESTURES.
– CONTROLLED STRETCHING CONTRASTED WITH BENDS.
– EXPANDING AND CONTRACTING ACTION.

You'll need to practise this many times.

BALLOON ON A STRING: Now you are standing. You are a balloon on a string, wanting to fly in all directions. Run forwards, run backwards in all directions.
Now you are bobbing around like a ball in the water. Stand with your feet apart. Step out in any direction and jump back to your place. Step out in any direction and jump back. Repeat with the other foot, and dance the same pattern. Dance these steps to the music **(BALLOONS, PART 2)**.

8

See photograph.

LOOK FOR:
– DEVELOPMENT OF STEP.
– CONTRAST: QUALITY OF BOUNCE AND JERK.
– SEQUENCE FLOW OF TRAVELLING FORWARDS AND BACKWARDS, STEPPING OUT/JUMPING BACK.
– DRAMATIC QUALITY.

THE BALLOON ESCAPES:

You pull so hard the string breaks, and away you float; spiralling, turning, spinning and bobbing. Travel quickly but lightly in a pattern that you like. Practise with the music **(BALLOONS, PART 3)**.

LOOK FOR:
– SLOW, SUSTAINED MOVEMENTS.
– INTERESTING TRAVEL PATTERNS AND DIRECTIONS.
– COMMAND OF THE SEQUENCE.

Link the whole dance together with the music: inflating the balloon, the balloon on a string, the balloon escaping.
(BALLOONS, ALL PARTS).

christmas

Christmas, Part 3 (dressed for an assembly): Children spell out the word *Christmas* in joined-up writing.

STIMULUS:	*A Christmas greeting card.*
DISCUSSION AND OBSERVATION:	Discuss how it was made, its design and colours used. Why was that message chosen? Discuss the meaning of Christmas, messages of the season, and cards the children have received for their birthdays. Discuss the art of calligraphy; show various styles of writing from around the world; Christmas greetings in various languages (*Christmas in the Primary School,* R. Brandling, Ward Lock Educational).
LANGUAGE:	Handwriting activities with pencil, pen, brush, quill. Alphabetical Christmas: anagrams of 'Christmas' and associated vocabulary. Study greetings in different languages and writing styles. Devise comprehension exercises developed from carols. Crosstick poetry from the word Christmas.
SCIENCE:	Jingle bells: • Arrange a selection of bells in order of pitch. • Make your own peal of bells using vessels of water.

MATHS: Enlarging: Write 'Merry Christmas' on small squared paper, work through stages of enlarging.
Gift boxes: study 3-dimensional shapes and their nets, decorate and make into gift boxes.
Study an assortment of star shapes; (e.g. compass work, building from triangles etc.) cut out, decorate, and hang as mobiles.

MULTICULTURAL: Christmas celebrations around the world.
Greetings in different languages.
Stories from around the world; 'Baboushka', (*Christmas in the Primary School*, R. Brandling, Ward Lock).

BOOKS: *Lucy & Tom's Christmas*, Shirley Hughes, Victor Gollancz Ltd.
Cider with Rosie, (carol singing scene), Laurie Lee, Penguin.
What a Mess in Winter, Frank Muir, Carousel.
Wind in the Willows, (Christmas Scene), Kenneth Grahame, Methuen.
Lettering and Typography, an Usborne Guide, Usborne Publishing Ltd.
Merry Christmas, Willson & Ichikawa, Heinemann.

POEMS: 'The Computer's First Christmas Card', Edwin Morgan, from *A Single Star: An Anthology of Christmas Poetry*, Bodley Head.
'The Christmas Tree', C. Day Lewis, from *A Single Star*, Bodley Head.

MUSIC: 'Christmas', Moriel Gidney, *Time to Dance* tape, Belair Publications Ltd.
'We wish you a Merry Christmas', trad., *Carol, Gaily Carol*,
A. & C. Black.
Merrily to Bethlehem, A. and C. Black.
'White Christmas', Irving Berlin.
'Christmas Album', compiled by EMI Records and Virgin Records Ltd.
'Musical Calendar of Festivals', B. Cass – Begges. Published by Ward Lock Educational.

ART AND CRAFT: Make Christmas cards with design of Christmas greetings in a variety of languages.
Illustration greetings: use the art of quilling to raise the letters; perhaps a group project for display in the classroom.
Textured messages: pipe plaster substitute on to card or balsa wood bases. Paint when dry.
Pastry messages: make pastry, cut out letters, arrange together, bake and varnish.
Stained glass messages: cut pictures, patterns and messages into black paper or card. Display against window with coloured tissue providing a stained glass effect. (See illustration).

WARM-UP: (Christmas is a kaleidoscope of customs and celebrations. Use these ideas in the warm-up. Ensure that the children stand with their feet apart, balanced and comfortable.)
Sway your shoulders from side to side, bending the supporting leg and stretching the other to allow your body to remain erect. Make the sway bigger and smaller like the Christmas bells ringing out. Clap your arms around your body, twisting from the trunk, as if you're out in the cold. Jump, pushing off from the balls of the feet, extending the ankles in the air, and land into a bend. Jump from two feet to two feet, two feet to one foot and one foot to one foot, as you try to get warm. Stretch to reach the six points of the star, tap each end.

―――――――――――― ● ――――――――――――

CHRISTMAS MESSAGE: Imagine you are lying in bed on Christmas morning. You are dreaming of presents. When the music plays, practise drawing the letters of 'Christmas' in the air, with different body parts; each part is a pen. Shake the whole body to show your excitement.
Draw "CH", shiver, "R", shiver, "IS", shiver, "T", shiver, "MAS" and shiver. Do this again, but use different parts of the body for each letter. Remember, letter, then shiver.
(CHRISTMAS, PART 1).
(Practise this section)

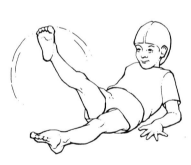

LOOK FOR:
– CONTROLLED USE OF THE BODY PARTS.
– THE ABSTRACT MOVEMENT HAS TO BE ENCOURAGED BY EMPHASISING THE UP, DOWN AND CURVED STROKES.
– DRAMATIC USE OF BODY WHEN SHIVERING.

CAPITAL LETTERS: Stand up, feet apart at a comfortable distance. Write each letter in capitals with your arms leading, using your whole body. Exaggerate each stroke: stretch, reach, curl, step, jump. Think about the starting place of each letter: does it have a push or a pull; start high, finish low. Do you have to move your feet?
Let's practise first without the music. Although the music is fast, your movement will be slower because it has been exaggerated, and each movement must be big to be seen. You must feel each letter as you move.
Now repeat this with the music. Keep writing until the music stops.
(CHRISTMAS, PART 2).

LOOK FOR:
– DYNAMICS OF TIME:
SOME LETTERS WILL HAVE
SLOW STRETCHES, BUT
QUICK JUMPS AND TRAVEL
STEPS.
– DYNAMICS OF SPACE:
SOME LETTERS WILL START
HIGH AND MOVE TO A
LOW LEVEL: DIRECT OR
INDIRECT.
– BODY ACTIONS:
STRETCH, CURL, TWIST,
STEP, JUMP.

CALLIGRAPHY:

Calligraphy is the study of handwriting styles. The flourish of the pen adds a loop, a curly tail, a dramatic pattern.
Carefully join each of your letter movements together, putting in a travelling gallop step, a kick, a twist or a turn; lead with an unusual part of the body.
Try first without the music. When you are ready, try with the music.
(CHRISTMAS, PART 3).

See photograph.

LOOK FOR:
– VARIATIONS IN TIME,
DIRECTION, BODY ACTION
AND EFFORT (FOR
EXAMPLE: 'C' – FEET
APART, STRETCH FROM
HIGH POSITION IN CURVED
PATHWAY TO THE SIDE.
THE REACH MEANS YOU
LEAN AWAY FROM THE
SUPPORTING LEG. SWAY
BACK ONTO THE OTHER
LEG, BUT GALLOP AWAY,
READY TO GO INTO THE
'H').

Link all three sequences: writing the word 'Christmas' lying down, then again while standing, and then in joined-up writing.
(CHRISTMAS, ALL PARTS).

clowns

Clowns, Part 3 (dressed for a special assembly): One clown walks the tightrope, while the other dances the heel-step movement.

STIMULUS: *A Jester playing-card or a clown doll.*

DISCUSSION AND OBSERVATION: Discuss the clothes and hat being worn. What is his job?
Why do we laugh at clowns?
Discuss the children's experiences of clowns.
Tell the story of Rahere, King Henry I's Court Clown who later became a monk and founded St. Bartholomew's Church and Hospital.

LANGUAGE: Describe a clown: dress, make-up, actions.
Explain how to juggle or tumble (any action in fact) without moving in any way. Audiences are allowed to ask questions.
Explore humour: jokes, puns, nonsense statements. Use books of Nonsense poetry (e.g. Spike Milligan's, *Milligan's Animals,* Puffin.)

HISTORY: Circus history.

Clown history:

The Auguste	– Egyptian clown
Grimaldi	– Italian clown
The Danga	– Ancient Egyptian clown
The Stupidus	– Roman clown
Pierrot	– French clown

Reference material can be found in:
'The Story of Clowns', Ladybird Books.
'The Circus', Elizabeth Cooper, Macdonald Educational.

14

P.E.:	Ball skills:

P.E.: Ball skills:
- Juggling, catching and throwing (individually/partner/groups)
- Throwing variously shaped and weighted objects to improve skill, i.e. wellington boots, bath sponges, cushions.

Gymnastics: tumbling safely, forward rolls, handstands etc.

BOOKS:
Quincy, Tommy Steele, Piccolo Books.
Angelo, Quentin Blake, Picture Puffins.
Nini at Carnival, Errol Lloyd, Picture Puffins.
Paddington at the Circus, Michael Bond, Collins.
The Clown of God, Tomie de Paola, Magnet.
The Know How Book of Jokes and Tricks, by Heather Amery and Ian Adair, Usborne Publishing Ltd.

POEMS:
'The Clown', from *Word Pictures as a Stimulus for Dance,* Edith Stokes, Macdonald & Evans Ltd.
Limericks, Michael Palin, Hutchinson.

MUSIC:
'Clowns', Moriel Gidney, *Time to Dance* tape, Belair Publications Ltd.
'The Clown', K. Blakeson and P. Canwell, *Appuskidu,* A. & C. Black.
Extracts from 'Barnum'.
Silent Movie Themes, BBC Tape.
'Flight of the Bumble-bee', Rimsky-Korsakov and other themes from 'Scheherazade'.
'Peer Gynt' by Greig, ('Hall of the Mountain King'.)

ART AND CRAFT:
Make a toy jester from a wooden spoon.
Design a jester or a pack of cards (collect a variety for observation).
Bottle clowns: paint empty plastic bottle with paint. Paint on a clown's face.
Clown mobile: Cut out clown's hat or hair and decorate both sides. Suspend from this two eyebrows and eyes. Suspend separately a nose, and from this a mouth. Add other items as wished. Ensure that the hat/hair is cut from heavy card. (See illustration).

WARM UP: Walk around the room without hurrying. Try to change the style of walking by making your step longer or shorter; by raising the knees or bending them; by stepping diagonally or cross-stepping. Always move with head held high. Think about the movement of your arms.

——————————— • ———————————

CLOWNS, PART 1:   With a partner, try each other's steps. Join up, one behind the other. The leader leads his partner through a series of different walks, changing when the music changes. Be clown-like, act mischievously. Then break away, walking backwards in a circle until you bump. The mock bump sends you both forward into a roll and into a sitting position.

Sit with your hands supporting your weight by resting on the floor behind. Lift your head and legs in unison: up, down, up down. Repeat the sequence to the end of the music.
(CLOWNS, PART 1).

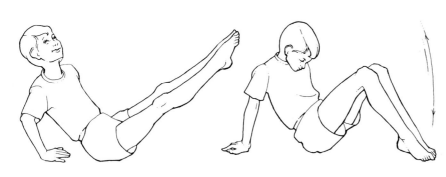

LOOK FOR:
– CLEARLY PERFORMED WALKING MOVEMENTS WITH CHANGES OF SPEED, TIME AND EFFORT.
– PARTNERSHIP: LEADING, FOLLOWING.
– CONTRAST BETWEEN HAPPY AND SAD MOVEMENTS OF LEGS AND HEAD.

CLOWNS, PART 2:   Lie on your back and bicycle in the air. Try to remember the feeling of the movement. Now stand and practise walking with the bicycle movement. You'll need to step with more bounce, tuck your legs up high and try not to go too fast. . .step, bicycle-skip, step etc.
Step and bicycle-skip in any direction, working with your partner. Check you are in unison. Travel backwards in your own circles and collide. The mock bump sends you rolling over, then stand up. Try this with the music until you are confident. Listen for the changes in the music.
(CLOWNS, PART 2).

Finish the music by standing and making the happy/sad gesture of a clown. First, head and hands up, knees and feet out. Then change by dropping head and arms, knees and feet turned in. Link all parts together. **(Repeat CLOWNS, PART 2).**

16

LOOK FOR:
– UNDERSTANDING OF CLOWN PARTNERSHIP.
– CHILDREN HAVING DIFFICULTIES WITH BICYCLE STEP.
– GOOD USE OF MUSIC AS STIMULUS.

CLOWNS, PART 3:

Step forward onto one heel, then onto the other heel. Step backwards with a bicycle-skip. Look clumsy, but do not overbalance. Now pretend to walk the tightrope, fall off, then roll over and stand up. Later the music will tell you when to leap and roll. Practise this first by yourself with the music. **(CLOWNS, PART 3).**

Perform this section with your partner. As one is walking the tightrope, the other is standing and doing the heel/step, then vice versa. **(Repeat CLOWNS, PART 3).**

The dance should finish with both clowns bumping into each other and falling down.

See photograph.

LOOK FOR:
– QUALITY OF HEEL STEP.
– THE TIGHTROPE WALK; FALL AND ROLL IS DANCED AND NOT ACTED. IT SHOULD BE SMOOTHLY LINKED TOGETHER.
– THE CLOWNS PERFORMING IN CONTRASTING WAYS, IN UNISON AND ONE AFTER THE OTHER.

Link all three sections together, clowns walking, clowns bicycling and clowns on the tightrope. **(CLOWNS, ALL PARTS).**

dragons

Dragons, Part 2 (costumed for a special occasion): The children sway as they are licked by the dragon.

STIMULUS:	*Junk model of a dragon.*
DISCUSSION AND OBSERVATION:	Discuss how the junk model was made, and why certain objects were used. Choose a name for the dragon; why that particular name? Show a picture of a lizard (or look at a live lizard). How does it move? What does it eat? How would the world look to a dragon? (Looking down on everyone, not enough food, being chased by knights in armour).
LANGUAGE:	Comprehension activities from stories of dragons and dinosaurs.
	Comparisons with modern-day 'dragons' — bulldozers, cranes, diggers etc.
	Drama: ● Re-enact the play George and the Dragon. ● Create own drama from the hymn 'When a Knight Won his Spurs'
	Vocabulary: ● Size-related words: large, lumbering, colossal. ● Emotive/descriptive words: fiercesome, terrible.
SCIENCE:	Study the life-cycles of dragonflies and newts.

HISTORY:	Dinosaurs: ● Timeline: put a chart around the wall — one child's foot print = 1 million years. ● Life histories — omnivore, carnivore, reptilian types. ● Evidence — fossils. ● Visit a natural history museum or nearest museum which has fossils.
MULTI-CULTURAL:	*Chinese New Year,* Ann Bancroft, Living Festival Series, Religious and Moral Educational Publishing. (In China the dragon is believed to be sacred and promises good fortune and power. It can change itself like a chameleon).
BOOKS:	*The Age of Dinosaurs,* David Lambert, Kingfisher Books, 1987. *Custard and Company,* Ogden Nash, Kestrel Books. *Green Smoke,* Rosemary Manning, Puffin Books. *How to draw Monsters and Other Creatures,* Cheryl Evans, Usborne Publications. *Danny and the Dinosaur,* Syd Hoff, A World's Work Children's Book. *Model a Monster,* Colin Caket, Blandford Press.
POEMS:	'Custard the Dragon', Ogden Nash, from *Once Upon a Rhyme,* Faber and Faber. 'Jocelyn, my dragon', Colin West, from *Rhyme Time 2,* Beaver Books. 'Be a Monster', Roy Fuller, from *A Second Poetry Book,* OUP. 'A Small Dragon', Brian Patten, from *Round about ten, poems for today,* Frederick Warne.
MUSIC:	'Dragons', Moriel Gidney, *Time to Dance* tape, Belair Publications Ltd. 'Dragon Boat' 20 Chinese Folksongs for Voice and Instrument, Chester Music. 'The Prehistoric Animal Brigade', *Okki-Tokki-Unga,* A. & C. Black. 'Puff the Magic Dragon', *Tinder-box,* A. & C. Black.
ART AND CRAFT:	Junk model of a dragon, individual or group effort. Shades of a dragon: cut out a large dragon from squared paper. Children paint in hot colours for the hot parts of a dragon and cold colours for the cold parts. Areas in between are painted in shades of the nearest colour (shades made by adding white). Mount on black, leaving 1 cm border. Arrange in a procession or formation. Models of dragons: Use paper plates, paper cups, doyleys and paper cases. Decorate with spatter paint, paper eyes, cottonwool smoke. Assemble. (See illustration).

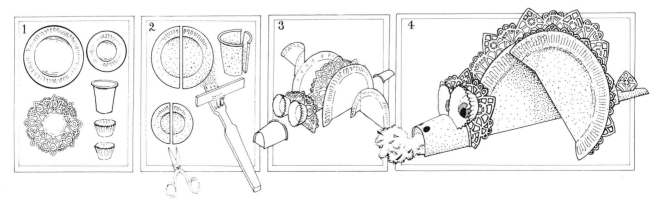

WARM-UP:

You're off to the sales. Walk quickly through the crowds of shoppers in the street. Change direction, don't bump into anyone. Stop, carefully cross the road. Off you go again. Pass the man who is digging a hole. Dig, dig with deep bends of the knees, good strong armwork. Travel on, past the woman hailing a taxi. Hail, with alternate arms, outstretched, standing on tip-toe. Finally, arrive at the doors of the shop. Pull them open and dart inside. Sit down on the floor.

——————————— • ———————————

THE MYSTERIOUS CREATURE:

The pet is a mysterious creature. To awaken it from its invisible sleep you first have to draw its shape in the air. Use your finger as a pencil and draw his outline, putting in all the details you can. Stand up.
Draw him again, as big as you can. Make him tall by jumping up to reach his head and ears. Now travel to the side as you draw his back, which is very very long and finishes at his tail. This is low down, near the ground. Let's repeat that: jump, stretching high; travel to the side; draw his back down to his tail.
Now use your hands to stroke him: stroke him from his head, down his back to his tail. Show me clearly what type of back he has. Is it smooth, lumpy or spiky? How can you show the difference? Maybe you could zig-zag your hand up and down. Jump or skip as you move along. Let's try and dance to the music. Make your pet appear before me.
(DRAGONS, PART 1).

LOOK FOR:
— CONCENTRATION WHILE DRAWING SMALL ANIMAL SHAPE (THIS HELPS TO DEVELOP FINE MOTOR SKILLS AND CO-ORDINATION).
— QUALITY OF BODY STRETCH (NOT STRAIN).
— CONTROLLED TRAVEL (RUNNING SHOULD BE GRACEFUL AND CONTROLLED. USE YOUR VOICE TO CUE START AND FINISH OF THE TRAVEL SEQUENCE).
— USE OF LEVELS (HIGH, MEDIUM AND LOW).
— TURN AND JUMP.

MEETING THE PET: After you have jumped for joy and run back to the head of the pet, look up. He has appeared. As he smiles, wave your hands. Cross them over above your head (as if you were trying to attract someone's attention). Do this quickly. The pet has a large tongue that begins to lick you. It is large but gentle, and makes you sway from side to side. Have your feet apart and as you sway try only to bend your knees, not move your feet. Listen to the next track. Make a pattern of waves and sways, in time with the music. **(DRAGONS, PART 2).**

See photograph.

LOOK FOR:
– SEQUENCE QUALITY
– CONTRAST OF STRONG RHYTHMIC WAVE AND SUSTAINED SWAYS.

LEASHING THE PET: As the pet is so special it needs a special lead. Place your feet apart, bend your knees and sink down ready to lift a golden collar and lead. Carefully, jump up and throw the collar over his head. Gather in the lead. Do this twice.
Hold the lead over your shoulder and lead him home. You'll have to take large strides: strides that look heavy but make no sound. You don't want to frighten him, do you.
Try this again, but as soon as you try to pull him, he pulls you in different directions, making you run. Pull him back with long heavy strides.
Listen to the music first, and then dance this sequence. **(DRAGONS, PART 3).**
End the dance by reaching up to stroke your pet, but look sad – he's vanished!

LOOK FOR:
– EFFORT QUALITY IN PICKING UP THE COLLAR AND LEAD.
– CONTRAST BETWEEN RUN/STRIDE.
– SEQUENCE DEVELOPMENT.
– SEQUENCE PERFORMANCE.

Link sequences one, two and three together with the music: draw the pet, stroke the pet to bring him alive; be licked by the pet; put on the collar and leash to take him home. He vanishes. **(DRAGONS, ALL PARTS).**

feeling angry

Feeling Angry, Part 1: The angry farmers stamp their feet when they find the broken machinery.

STIMULUS: *Extract from "The Iron Man", Ted Hughes, Faber and Faber.*

DISCUSSION AND OBSERVATION: What makes you angry? What do you do? How do you act? Do you do the same when you're happy, sad, or hurt? How can you tell when someone else is angry: your mother, or a man in the street? Find an assortment of pictures illustrating various emotions.

LANGUAGE: Drama: Given situations, e. g. 'saying sorry', 'becoming angry', 'feeling jealous'.

Vocabulary:
• Words to describe each emotion.
• Similes — as angry as a growling bear, as calm as the sea.

Sentence building: cause and effect — 'she is angry because. .'

Write poems built on the colours of emotions — 'seeing red', 'green with jealousy'.

'Love is' cartoons — develop simple sentences about emotions: love, anger, jealousy.

22

SCIENCE:	Make a study of muscles and try related experiments (e.g. strength tests).
	Discuss adrenalin: the hormone of fright, flight and fight. Talk about behaviour patterns: Why does a rabbit freeze in the light beam of a car?
	Find out about different forms of camouflage.
MULTI-CULTURAL:	Apostles John 2, Verse 12-16 and Matthew 21, Verse 12 (Jesus in the Temple).
BOOKS:	*Angry Arthur,* Hiawyn Oram, Picture Puffins. *Bottersnikes and Gumbles,* S. A. Wakefield, Piccolo Books. *My Mate Shofiq,* Jan Needle, Armada Books. *The Iron Man,* Ted Hughes, Faber and Faber. *Skiffy,* William Mayne, Hamish Hamilton. *How to Draw Cartoons and Caricatures,* Judy Tatchell, Usborne Publishing Ltd.
POEMS:	'When I get angry', Linda Newsham from *Fresh Voices,* N.C.E.C. 'Jabberwocky', Lewis Carroll. 'Fear', Barbara Ireson, from *Rhyme Time 2,* Beaver Books. 'Who's Scared Now', Max Fatchen, from *Rhyme Time 2,* Beaver Books. 'The Longest Journey in the World', Michael Rosen, from *The Second Poetry Book,* OUP.
MUSIC:	'Feeling Angry', Moriel Gidney, *Time to Dance* tape, Belair Publications Ltd. 'Fight', from *West Side Story,* L. Bernstein.
ART AND CRAFT:	Make a collage of shapes related to an emotion: red angry shapes, white calm shapes, green jealous shapes.
	Paint a picture of emotional scene, perhaps illustrating extract from a story.
	Draw portraits of faces showing all emotions, and develop into study of cartoon characters. (See illustration).

WARM-UP: Follow me as I trot and hop about the room. Now, skip into a space and sit down, backs straight, not curved or arched. Make your shoulders trot and skip, your knees jog, but keep your feet still. Think about your elbows; make them skip around you. Jump up, and skip once more in all directions.

———————————— ● ————————————

ANGRY FARMER: First of all, you are a farmer, very angry because he has found that his machinery has been broken. When you're angry you stamp your feet and shake your fist. Try it. Stamp your feet and shake your fist. Turn around and stamp your feet and shake your fist in another direction. Do it again, but don't let me hear the stamp. Pretend to stamp heavily, but at the last moment gently put your foot down. Try this with the music, walking in a figure of eight, stamping, shaking your fist and your head. **(FEELING ANGRY, PART 1).**

See photograph.

LOOK FOR:
– ANGRY QUALITY OF STAMPING.
– TRAVELLING IN A FIGURE OF EIGHT.
– USE OF HEAD AND FIST.
– ACCURATE PERFORMANCE WITH THE MUSIC.

FRIGHTENED PEOPLE: Now you are the frightened people.
Stand on the balls of your feet and look up. You are shaking with fear; the angry farmer has seen you. You tremble your fingers, elbows, legs and shoulders. Tremble all over. He makes you jump high and twitch with fear. A twitch is a very sharp movement, as if you're flicking away a fly. Try this movement with the music. It will tell you when to tremble and when to jump and twitch. **(FEELING ANGRY, PART 2).**

LOOK FOR:
– TREMBLING MOVEMENT THAT TRAVELS UP THROUGH ALL PARTS AND USES ALL PARTS.
– TWITCHING GESTURE WHICH IS SHARP AND NOT NECESSARILY MADE WITH HANDS – ENCOURAGE USE OF BODY PARTS.

THE BROKEN MACHINERY:

Listen to the music. Can you hear the broken machinery? Wheels are spinning, mudguards rocking, odd shapes of machinery are lying around. **(FEELING ANGRY, PART 3).**

Make yourself into an uncomfortable, broken shape. How can you move? Can you rock, tip and spin? Can you link three different movements together? **(FEELING ANGRY, PART 3).**

LOOK FOR:
– A VARIETY OF MOVEMENTS THAT SLOWLY COME TO A STOP.
– USE OF STILLNESS.
– DIFFERENT WAYS OF SPINNING.
– QUALITY OF SEQUENCE.

Link the three sections, the angry farmer, the frightened people, and the broken machinery. **(FEELING ANGRY, ALL PARTS).**

fireworks

Fireworks, Part 3 (dressed for a special assembly): Rockets shoot upwards into the air during the fireworks display.

STIMULUS: *A fireworks display or a picture of a display.*

DISCUSSION AND OBSERVATION: Discuss each statement of the Firework Code, their implications and consequences.
How do fireworks make the children feel, and what do they remind them of?
Discuss the use of fireworks in celebrations.
Listen to Handel's Royal Firework Music.

LANGUAGE: Creative writing:
- Use poetry about fireworks to stimulate writing (for example, the Fireworks Section, in *The Third Poetry Book*, John Foster, Oxford University Press).
- 'A pet's view of fireworks'.

Onomatopoeic work from words like whoosh, whoop, whee, whizz, zizz, phtt. (Mount descriptive work on star-shaped paper to display with artwork).

Use the Fireworks Code for comprehension tasks.

HISTORY:	The story of Guy Fawkes and the Gunpowder Plot.
MULTI-CULTURAL:	The Firework Story – inventions by the Chinese in the 9th Century as a result of the discovery of gunpowder.
BOOKS:	*Firework Party,* Peggy Blakeley, A. & C. Black. Extract from *Mary Poppins Opens the Door,* P. L. Travers, Collins. *Festivals,* compiled by Ruth Manning Saunders, Heinemann.
POEMS:	'Fireworks', from *Once Upon a Rhyme,* Faber and Faber. 'A Box of Fireworks', Wes Magee, from *A Third Poetry Book,* OUP. 'Bonfire', Alexander Resnikoff, from *A Third Poetry Book,* OUP. 'Gunpowder Plot', Vernon Scannell, from *A Flock of Words,* collected by David Mackay, The Bodley Head.
MUSIC:	'Fireworks', Moriel Gidney, *Time to Dance* tape, Belair Publications Ltd. 'Royal Firework Music', Handel. 'Slavonic Dances', Opus 46, Dvorak.
ART AND CRAFT:	Paintings: Wash paper with water. Drop water colour paint on with pipette or straw. Watch how paint 'explodes'. Allow to dry. Paint or cut silhouette of rooftops and mount along the bottom. (For added effect: drop salt or sugar on to the wet painting. Brush off when dry.) Use fluorescent crayons to draw pictures of fireworks party and bonfire. Overwash with thin blue paint to make into night scene. Class display of 3-dimensional rockets, streamers and stars. Mount as in illustration. Star shapes could be suspended from ceiling, to hang just in front of display. (See illustration)

WARM-UP:

Lead an exercise of 'following my leader': quick routine of skips, hops, stretches, involving all levels; contrasted with a slow routine of twists and turns on the spot.

———————————— • ————————————

ROCKETS:

In all good firework displays, as one firework fades, another is bursting, and others are just taking off. The sky is busy with sounds and trails of light: flickering, fading stars and the sudden bang of an explosion. To capture the atmosphere our dance must be busy. Sit down and listen to the music. **(FIREWORKS, PART 1).**
To begin, crouch with your feet slightly apart and your body balanced by resting on your fingers: spread and raise them to take the weight. Bounce cautiously; with a low push spring into the air. Spread into a star shape. Do this several times and then *slowly* flicker the hands and fade the star shape down into a crouch ready to start again.
Dance this sequence with the music **(Repeat FIREWORKS, PART 1).**

LOOK FOR:
— QUALITY AND CONTRAST BETWEEN SUDDENNESS OF ROCKET MOVEMENT AND FLICKERING OF STARS
— RISING ROCKET JUMP: AND SINKING, FADING STAR.
— THE FEELING FOR MUSIC RHYTHM.
— PERFORMANCE QUALITY OF SEQUENCE.

THE JUMPING FIREWORKS:

Some fireworks travel sideways, jumping from place to place. Some jump sideways along the ground.
Stand with your feet slightly apart, knees bent and elbows tucked into the side. Stretch your hands to the tips of the fingers. Walk sideways like this. Step to the right with the right foot, cross over the left; step right, cross left, step right onto ball of foot and stretch out into a star shape. Try the same stepping sequence to the left. When the music tells you, flicker and fade as you did before. Practise with the music **(FIREWORKS, PART 2).**

LOOK FOR:
— DIRECT PATHWAY TRACED WITH SIDE STEPPING.
— QUALITY OF STRETCH: THE EFFORT COMING FROM THE CENTRE OF THE BODY.
— USE OF HEAD TO SUGGEST DRAMA.
— AN UNDERSTANDING THAT REPETITION OF FLICKERING, FADING MOVEMENT ADDS TO THE DYNAMICS OF THE DANCE.

Practise Sections 1 and 2.

THE DISPLAY:

To make the dance look busy, we need to show the direct trails of the shooting rockets, the twirling Catherine Wheels and the falling stars. Let one hand shoot upwards, keeping it and the arm straight, allowing it to pull you onto the balls of the feet. The back of the hand leads you into a run and as the hand flickers and falls to the ground, so the run slows down. Your hands shoot upwards as many times as you wish, then follow another pathway whenever you feel the need.

Practise with the music. Use all the music. **(FIREWORKS, PART 3).**

Now, let's turn like a Catherine Wheel. Put out your hand, palm upwards, as if you are making friends with a dog. Your palm leads your body in a circle, turning on the spot. Keep your chest open and move smoothly. Lower or raise your arms and head as you turn. Do the opposite when you turn the other way.

Practise this whole section: first, rocket hands shooting upwards and out, travelling through the air and flickering and fading; Catherine Wheels, spiralling and turning, ending by fading. **(Repeat FIREWORKS, PART 3).**

See photograph.

LOOK FOR:
— OPPORTUNITIES TO ADD MORE DYNAMICS: USE OF THE HEAD, CHANGE OF SPEED, CHANGE OF DIRECTIONS; FORMATIONS AND USE OF JUMPS.
— ACCURATE USE OF LEADING HAND IN THE TURN.
— CONTRAST BETWEEN DIRECT UPWARD THRUST AND WIDE SPREADING TURN.

Link the three sections together: the rockets, the jumping fireworks, and the fireworks display. **(FIREWORKS, ALL PARTS).**

flight

Flight, Part 3 (dressed for an assembly): The kites begin to sink and fall to the ground.

STIMULUS:	*Poster of a bird flying, or a kite, or a 'Wanted' poster.*
DISCUSSION AND OBSERVATION:	Flight has two meanings: the act of flying, especially birds, and the act of fleeing, or hasty departure. Have you ever run away from something or someone? Have you seen a bird fly? How does it fly? What else flies? Watch a kite as it dances in the wind. What does it use to fly? Winds, engine design?
LANGUAGE:	Creative writing: • 'A Bird's Eye View' • 'The Journey' • 'Icarus (the story retold by children after hearing the story.) Vocabulary: • Collect all flight-associated words: soar, glide, flap, beat, hover, swoop. • Collect all words associated with fright: chase, scared, petrified.
SCIENCE:	Discuss parachutes, kites, balloons, gliders, darts.

Design experiments related to aerodynamics and trajectory.

Investigate seed dispersal by the wind — related designs in nature.

Study the design of a bird's wing; elements of flight.

HISTORY:
Flight: from Icarus to the Jet.
Evolution of birds.
The Wright Brothers

MULTI-CULTURAL:
Songkran Festival: (kite-flying celebrations) from *Festivals of the Buddha*, Anne Bancroft, Living Festival Series, Religious and Moral Education Pub.

The Flight from Israel — Exodus Chapter 14, Verses 8–10, New Testament Bible.

BOOKS:
Charlotte's Web, E. B. White (extract — baby spiders dispersed on threads of silk), Hamish Hamilton.
The Carnival Kite, Grace Hallworth, Methuen.
Up and up, Shirley Hughes, Bodley Head.
Fun with Kites, John and Kate Dyson, Angus & Robertson, Publishers.
I am David, Anne Holme, Methuen.

POEMS:
'Bird and Boy', Leslie Norris, from *A Third Poetry Book*, OUP.
'To a red kite', Lilian Moore, from *Rhyme Time 2*, Beaver Books.
'Feel Like a Bird', May Swenson, from *Junior Voices, the Second Book*, Penguin Educational.
'How do you like to go up in a swing?' Robert Louis Stevenson, *From Morn to Midnight*, chosen by E. Moss, Heinemann.

MUSIC:
'Flight', Moriel Gidney, *Time to Dance* tape, Belair Publications Ltd.
'Flight of the Bumble Bee', Rimsky-Korsakov.

ART AND CRAFT:
Life drawings of birds, settled and in flight.

Record a bird's flight patterns. Draw on large pieces of paper, cut out along lines (they dip and weave). Mount one over the other in collage form.

Make flicker books of birds in flight or diving.

Free painting, entitled 'What am I running from?'

Make simple kites. Draw other more complicated kites. (See illustration)

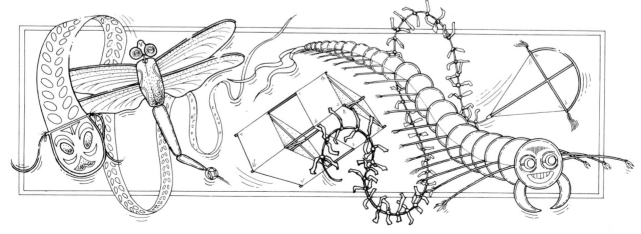

WARM-UP: Lie on the floor with your knees bent and the soles of the feet flat on the floor. Tap your feet and beat on the floor gently with the palms of your hands. Rock from side to side, bringing your knees to touch the floor. Roll over onto your feet. Crouch on the balls of the feet and gently bounce.

Keep your legs bouncing, but gently stand up. Try to lead from the top of your head. As you move upwards think about walking upstairs, ending up on the balls of your feet. Walk downstairs, go through various levels, bending your knees to finally stop in a crouch.

———————————— • ————————————

THE TAKE OFF: Stand with your feet apart, and bend your knees slightly. Launch yourself upward into the air, land gently, bending the knees, landing on the balls of the feet and allowing the action to pass through your feet until your heels touch the floor. Try this again. Try to touch the sky as you leap.

Pretend you're a kite being launched, then suddenly caught by the wind.

Each time you leap make a new gesture with your arms and head, remembering to land safely and lightly. Link jumps together and end with a short run of a few steps, as if you're taking off. Try the jumps and runs with the music **(FLIGHT, PART 1).**

LOOK FOR:
– RESPONSE TO COMMANDS.
– GOOD LANDING POSITIONS.
– IMAGINATIVE GESTURES AND SHAPES.
– CONTROLLED FORWARD TRAVEL.

IN FLIGHT:

Now you are free to fly like a kite. Show me how proud you are to be flying: open out your arms, throw your head back and let your chest lead you forward. Stand on the balls of your feet, gently tip forward and then run away. The kite dips as if to fall, but rises in the wind. Practise this balance and the slow tipping forward which makes you run in any direction or pathway.

Listen to the music: it glides and soars like your movement. Try with the music. **(FLIGHT, PART 2).**

LOOK FOR:
— WIDE OPEN GESTURES.
— CONTROLLED TRAVELLING STEPS.
— A STILL BALANCE.
— GOOD USE OF ARMS.
— SEQUENCE OF DEVELOPMENT.
— AWARENESS OF MUSIC.

GOING TO GROUND:

The kite begins to fall as the wind drops. Slowly, very slowly, take a step forward onto the right leg, bending both knees. Going down onto the left knee, keeping bottom tucked in and the back straight, allow yourself to gently collapse onto the floor and roll to the side. Practise this. It is very slow.

Collapse and roll right over, coming back onto the balls of your feet. Stand up, ready to begin again. Let's try this with the music. **(FLIGHT, PART 3).**

See photograph.

LOOK FOR:
— CONTRAST OF STRETCH/ BENDS.
— THE QUALITY OF THE ROLL.
— SEQUENCE DEVELOPMENT.

Now link all three sections and perform the whole dance to the music, the take off, in flight, and going to ground. **(FLIGHT, ALL PARTS).**

33

hornpipe

Hornpipe, Part 3: The sailors climb the rigging, look out from the crow's nest and salute the **captain**.

STIMULUS: *Pictures from 'The Fisherman', a Ladybird Easy-Reading book, 'People at Work' series.*
OR a picture postcard from the seaside.

DISCUSSION/ OBSERVATION: Fishing is very tiring work. Fishermen have to haul in their nets, and row the dinghy out to the boats. Can you see any other people in the picture who are working hard? What are they doing? Draw attention to the action involved. Analyse it, copy it. Discuss how the group of fishermen work together.

LANGUAGE: Creative writing:
- Shipwrecked.
- Message in a bottle.
- Diary of a press-ganged sailor.

Sayings and superstitions related to work: e.g. Red sky at night, Sailors' delight. (Discuss why sayings may have arisen).

'I spy through the telescope' — classroom activity with the task of finding things in alphabetical order.

'I spy in a picture' — visual discrimination.

Verbal comprehension: study of picture and discussion of what is happening.

SCIENCE: Design a ship. Discuss ballast, cargo loading, floating and sinking, the plimsoll line — related experiments.

Salt-water experiments: investigate evaporation and condensation.

34

The water cycle: from the mountains to the sea; from the tank to the tap; from the drain to the sewerage plant.

Life in a drop of water: use microscopes after a pond-dipping exercise.

Discuss the body's need for water.

HISTORY:
History of the fishing fleet: trawling, drifting, netting.
Naval history: famous sailors, battles, voyages, pressgangs and sailors.

MULTI-CULTURAL:
Christian stories related to fish and fishing:
'Jonah and the Whale'
'Feeding the Five Thousand'

BOOKS:
Treasure Island, R. L. Stevenson, Longman.
Moonfleet, J. Meade Falkner, Heinemann Educational.
Hornblower series, C. S. Forester, Penguin.
See Inside a Galleon, Ed. R. J. Unstead, Kingfisher Books.

POEMS:
'When my Dad came Home from the Sea', Ian McMillan, from *Marbles in My Pocket,* Macmillan.
'Pirate Captain Jim', from *A Third Poetry Book,* OUP.
'I do like to be beside the Seaside', John A. Glover-Kind, from *The Puffin Book of Salt-Sea Verse,* Kestrel Books.
'The Tide Rises, the Tide falls', H. W. Longfellow, from *Fancy Free,* Evans Bros. Ltd.

MUSIC:
'Hornpipe', Moriel Gidney, *Time to Dance* tape, Belair Publications Ltd.
'My Ship Sailed from China', trad., *Appuskidu,* A. & C. Black Ltd.
Sea shanties.

ART AND CRAFT:
Knot pictures:
- Follow instructions for various knots.
- Make knots in various types of wool, string, cotton, to add to a collage.
- Sketch the lines of knot strands as seen through a magnifying glass.

Paintings entitled "Through the telescope": circular paper with horizon given. Discuss perspective. ('a seascape' or 'sea creatures').

Three dimensional fish: cut flat shape. Make one straight cut into middle. Fix edges by overlapping them to give fish a curve. Decorate fish and glue onto painted backing. (See illustration)

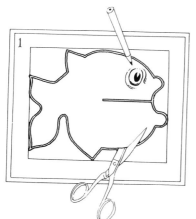
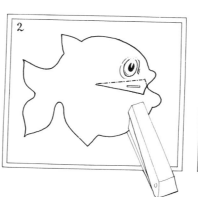
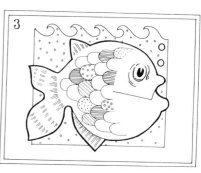

WARM-UP:
Imagine you're at the edge of the sea. Kick and splash the water. Now gently just kick the water. Feel your foot gliding into the water and jerking out. Ssssh, don't make a sound. Gently again. Now, let's jump over the tiny waves, jump, jump many times. Jump higher, but land in the same place. Repeat. Finally, let's jump the waves and kick and splash all around.
Now skip back to your towels and lie down.

————————— • —————————

HAULING UP THE ANCHOR AND SAILS:
We're going back in time to the days of sailing ships. The sailors are marched up the gangplank in a straight line. Come on, quick march. Now they put down their sacks and get ready to haul the anchor. Feet apart, one foot in front of the other. Hands out-stretched, hold the rope and pull it towards your chest. Sink into a bend at the same time and release by jumping up and backwards. Pause slightly before the next one.
Next they have to haul up the sails. This is just like pulling up the anchor, only the rope hangs down. You have to pull down on the rope, one hand after the other. Try to do this. Pull and pull, pull and pull. Now try skipping on the spot at the same time.
Try this with the music, marching, then hauling the anchor and then the sails. **(HORNPIPE, PART 1).**

LOOK FOR:
– QUALITY OF WALK.
– USE OF BENDS, KNEES, ANKLES AND TOE JOINTS TO SUGGEST CLEAR, DIRECT EFFORT WHEN HAULING.
– STRETCH OF ARMS IN 'ANCHOR AND SAIL' STEP.
– ENCOURAGE THE ABSORPTION OF THE BOUNCE IN THE MUSIC BY SKIPPING, TAPPING OR LIGHTLY CLAPPING YOURSELF.

UNDER SAIL:

The boat rocks from side to side. Stand on one leg and cross the other over at the ankles. Gently rock from foot to foot. Practice this. Now try to bend your knees slightly to help the movement, and fold your arms. Look relaxed, shoulders down.

Listen to the music, and rock in time. **(HORNPIPE, PART 2).**

As the music carries on, jump down onto the floor. Sailors have to scrub the decks while under sail. They go down onto their knees, holding the brush with both hands, backwards and forwards they scrub – moving in all directions. Try to scrub in time with the music, making patterns on the floor that you repeat.

Let's try the whole sequence again, rocking steps and scrubbing steps. Here's the music again. **(Repeat HORNPIPE, PART 2).**

LOOK FOR:
– CORRECT BODY POSITIONS AND TENSIONS: NO SCRUNCHED SHOULDERS: ALL THE POWER FOR THE BEND AND JUMP COMES FROM THE LEGS.
– RHYTHMIC ROCKING (CLAP TO EMPHASISE PATTERN).
– OPPORTUNITIES TO REALLY OUTSTRETCH AND EXTENDS LIMBS.
– DYNAMIC CHANGE OF ACTION WHEN MUSIC CALLS FOR IT.

WORKING RHYTHM:

What else did sailors do? They climbed the rigging, looked out from the crow's nest, saluted the captain and walked the plank! Dance with a skip, one of these actions. You have four slow counts for every movement.

Listen to the last piece of the music. Now perform your working step. **(HORNPIPE, PART 3).**

See photograph.

LOOK FOR:
– QUALITY OF STEP.
– THE TYPE OF ACTION AND HOW IT FITS INTO THE MUSIC.

Link the three sequence together with the music:
1. March onto the ship and haul the anchor.
2. Hoist the sail, rock and scrub.
3. Work to the rhythm and then end in a very still pose, suggesting a photograph. **(HORNPIPE, ALL PARTS).**

light (divali)

Light (Divali) Part 2 – dressed for a special assembly: The children move in a rhythmic skating action, representing Rama following Ravana.

STIMULUS:	*The Story of Rama (e.g. "Celebrations – Diwali", Beulah Candappa, Ginn & Co. Ltd.)*
DISCUSSION AND OBSERVATION:	Light a candle. Why does it make us feel good? Why is the dark frightening? What shadows can you make? What colours can you see in a flame? Explain the difference between torchlight and candlelight. Where do we get natural light from?
LANGUAGE:	Creative writing: 'The story of a fire' – strike a match or light a small fire outside.
	Light is an abstract representation of good. Discuss Good 'n' Bad stories such as Cinderella. Write your own Fairy Tales.
	Vocabulary: Words associated with light – glare, beam, shine.
	Names of lights collected: flashlight, striplight, spotlight, glowlight, headlight, searchlight.
	Use as a subject for poetry.
SCIENCE/MATHS:	Light sources: the sun, electricity, fire, candles. Shadows and related mathematical experiments: e.g. sundials, lengths of shadows. Camouflage; the senses; the eye; the camera; colour. The sun and Equinox; tides; the calendar.

HISTORY:
Lighthouses (navigational aids).
Heating in the home.
Electricity in the home.
Inventions and discoveries (i.e. electric light bulb – Joseph Swan in England, and Thomas Edison in the United States).
History through the camera: make a photographic display.

MULTI-CULTURAL:
Diwali – Hindu Festival of Light, Howard Marsh, Living Festival Series R.M.E.P.
Shabbat – Jewish Celebration, Christopher Bryan and Victor Whitburn, Living Festival Series, R.M.E.P.
Ramadan – Muslim Festival, Janis Hannaford, Living Festival Series, R.M.E.P.
Channuka: Jewish Festival of Light
Advent, Christmas, Epiphany: Christian Festivals

BOOKS:
The Story of Prince Rama, Brian Thomson, Viking Kestrel.
Hanuman, A. Ramachandran, A. and C. Black.
Marianne Dreams, Catherine Storr, Hardy Books.

POEMS:
'The Menlips', J. R. R. Tolkien.
'A light in the dark: An anthology of poetry' from the BBC Radio Production, *Pictures in your mind.*
Many light-related poems in *Poetry 1, 2 and 3,* Macmillan.

MUSIC:
'Divali', Moriel Gidney, *Time to Dance* tape, Belair Publications Ltd.
'Divali', *Tinder-box,* A. & C. Black.
'Sun Arise', *Tinder-box,* A. & C. Black.

ART/CRAFT:
Candle-wax paintings.

Silhouettes – use a projector to make large silhouettes of child. Partner draws around outline. Class montage.

Photography – use light sensitive paper. Place grasses and flowers, then expose to light. When removed, photograph is left.

Make and use pinhole camera.

Experiment with colour tints and shades.

Look at traditional Indian pictures and patterns. Draw the outlines, then decorate with different seeds and/or powder paints. (See illustration)

WARM-UP:
Imagine you are waiting on tables in a restaurant. You have to serve the food. The tray is on your hand, held up above your head. Keep it level. Gently but quickly weave in and out around the room. Dip and weave, rise and sink. Lead with your left and right arm alternately. Make it obvious when you have to squeeze by some chairs.
Now sweep the floor, turn the chairs over onto the tables, and put all your effort into it.

———————————— • ————————————

INDIAN CHORUS:
The Divali story comes from India, so our dance needs to have an Indian style.
Stand with your feet slightly apart. Remembering to remain on the spot, fake one gesture of presenting a tray. Go through the movement slowly. Where does your hand lead? Where does your hand start and finish?
Repeat that but exaggerate the movement so it is really very big. Keep the hand flat. Do the same with the other arm but bring your hands back to a praying position.
Now I want you to make your right foot follow the right hand's gesture. Come back to the starting position. Repeat with the left. Do this again, to the right and left. This makes one phrase of movement.
Now make your hands dance in another way to make a second gesture, and in another way.
Dance these three ideas one after another. We'll call it the chorus.
(DIVALI, PART 1)

LOOK FOR:
– MOVEMENT'S DIRECTION: WHERE DOES IT LEAD? HOW DOES IT FINISH?
– EXTENSIVE USE OF GRACEFUL HANDS.
– USE OF STILLNESS AND BALANCE.
– USE OF ANY BEND.

(The sequence should be fluid and suggest elegance, and the body shouldn't move.)

TRAVELLING MOVEMENT:

(In the following action Rama is following Ravana to Sri Lanka.)
Skate in every direction – either ice skate or roller skate. Slow the action down. You swing your arms from side to side and your legs must travel diagonally. Where does your body lean? What is your head doing? Can you make the movement end in a roll, by sliding to the floor, rolling over and standing up, ready to start again. Repeat this to the end of the music phrase. **(DIVALI, PART 2)**

See photograph.

LOOK FOR:
– USE OF ARMS, LEGS, HEAD AND BODY IN SLIDING GESTURE.
– CONTRAST OF GLIDING SLIDE AND SPIKY ROLL.

WORKING RHYTHM:

Practise sweeping the floor. Now dig a hole, wash up, lift a heavy object, smash a rock or chop wood. These actions need effort.
Bend your knees and use deliberate, exaggerated movements to illustrate the action, but do not strain. Choose one such action and practise. While you are performing, can you put in an unusual gesture? For example, allow your hammer to bounce twice, your hand to draw a circle, or your head to nod twice. Make sure your body is being used in a balanced way. Don't do everything with the one side. Repeat the movement with the other side.
Perform these working actions with the music. This sequence represents Hanuman's army building the bridge. **(DIVALI, PART 3).**

LOOK FOR:
– WORKING RHYTHM.
– HEAVY SUSTAINED ACTION.
– USE OF BENDS (SINKING/ RISING)
– EXTENSION OF LIMBS.

Listen to the music and perform the whole dance, linking the Indian Chorus, the skating sequence and the working rhythms. **(DIVALI, ALL PARTS).**

41

new clothes

New Clothes, Part 3: The children in their new clothes swirl, flutter and drift like snowflakes.

STIMULUS: *Make a display of new items of clothing, pieces of dress pattern and dressmaking equipment, e.g. a sewing machine.*

DISCUSSION: Look at the new clothing. Discuss how it was made: pattern, pieces, stitches, buttons. Discuss what happens after they have been made: from the factory to the shop.
Talk about fashion advertising. Look at advertisement examples.
Why might you have new clothes?
Discuss different types of clothes: special clothes, uniforms, national costumes, clothes for different seasons.

LANGUAGE: Arrange a fashion show (comic or serious): children write descriptions of clothes, perform, and act as presenters.

Comprehension exercises: children read or listen to a description of clothes and then draw what is described.

(Infants: sort out materials: textures, colours. Develop vocabulary.)

SCIENCE: Material tests:
- Wash and dry clothes in various weathers — time, and record graphically.
- Wear and tear test — devise own test for staining, tearing and strength.

Microscope work: Look for warp and weft.

Study sewing machine mechanics.

HISTORY: Study clothes fashions of 20th Century as they relate to dance trends: Charleston — the fringed dress and Oxford bags; ballroom gowns and court dances; Rock 'n' Roll jeans and pumps.

42

MULTI-CULTURAL: National costumes:
- Display costumes from different cultures.
- Display dolls in national dress.
- Have a national costume day.

Arrange for demonstration of national dances.

Show how costumes (e.g. sari) are worn.

MATHS: Set the task of children ordering a complete outfit from a clothing catalogue: include fitting/measuring, ordering/pricing.

Calculate area from clothes patterns.

BOOKS: *Costumes and Clothes,* Jean Cooke, Wayland (Pub.) Ltd., 1986.
Doing the Washing, Sarah Garland, Picture Puffins.
The Emperor's New Clothes, Ladybird Books.
The Shoemaker and the Elves, Ladybird Books.
The Wild Washerwomen, John Yeoman, Picture Puffins.
How do people dress, Macdonald & Co.
A Parcel of Patterns, Jill Paton Walsh, Puffin Plus.

POEMS: 'New Shoes', John Agard, from *I Din Do Nuttin!,* Bodley Head.
'Stocking and Shirt', James Reeves, from *Once Upon a Rhyme,* Faber and Faber.
'Clothes', Elizabeth Jenning from *A Second Poetry Book,* OUP.

MUSIC: 'New Clothes', Moriel Gidney, *Time to Dance* tape, Belair Publications Ltd.
'Joseph and the Amazing Technicolour Dreamcoat', Andrew Lloyd Webber.
'In Dulce Jubilo', Mike Oldfield.

ART AND CRAFT: Use old clothes to make hot water bottle covers, peg bags, scarecrows.

Print material: tie 'n' dye, simple batik, fabric paints.

Calendars: children design an outfit to represent each month of the year. Assemble with small calendar.

Design a new outfit: Figure is cut from thick cardboard and used as a template for drawing clothes. Small pieces of Velcro are glued to front of figure and underside of clothes so they can be fitted and removed easily. Figure should be glued onto heavy card base or weighted matchbox as shown. Cut slots into hats to fit over head. (See illustration)

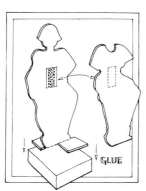

WARM-UP:

(Each child holds a scarf or piece of material).
Stand still, with feet apart. Flick the scarf in all directions, trying to reach the furthest points. Change hands. Avoiding anyone else, run into a space, pause, stretch and flick.
Hold both ends of your scarf, using your two hands. Pull it in all directions as if the hands were arguing. Throw the scarf into the air, and watch how it settles. Repeat this, and as it settles, you try to follow it to the ground.

———————————————— • ————————————————

CUTTING THE CLOTH:

Stand with feet placed a little way apart. Brush your hands together, as if they are very dusty. Make the action bigger, bigger, as if you're playing the cymbals.
Make a similar action with your legs and feet without them touching. You'll need to bounce gently; legs straight, stretching your ankles so your toes are pointed. Try and travel forward with this scissor step, making the step much wider.
Travel in a set pathway, cutting out the pattern for your new clothes. Change your scissor step to fast but tiny little tiptoe steps, as you sew around your material. Use your hands to lead you up and down through the material. Travel the same pathway again.
Use these steps to make a dance, alternating between cutting and sewing. Use all the music in Part 1. (NEW CLOTHES, PART 1).

LOOK FOR:
– A CONTRAST BETWEEN WIDE OPEN SCISSOR STEPS AND TINY LITTLE STITCHES.
– AN INTERESTING PATHWAY, CORRECTLY REPEATED.
– WELL HELD BODY AND HEAD.
– QUIET, CONTROLLED LANDING.

PUTTING ON NEW CLOTHES:

Practise getting dressed. Slowly step into a trouser leg; bend forward and pull your hands forward from the ankles, up through your body and push them out into the air. Are you in a stretched diagonal line? Repeat with other leg.
Stretch an arm upward diagonally, into the arm of a jumper. Stretch and rise onto your toes. Repeat with other arm. Practise slow stretches with the music. (NEW CLOTHES, PART 2).

44

The music has slow and quick phrases. Build a sequence of slow dressing followed by quick actions: slow stretches, quick bounces and stretches.

Develop the sequence by stretching the arms out sideways, and as you continually turn on the spot, bring your arms in as if they are a scarf being wrapped around. Practise with the music. **(Repeat, NEW CLOTHES, PART 2).**

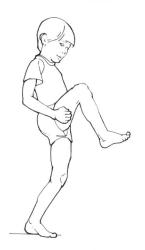 

LOOK FOR:
— CONTRAST OF STRETCH AND BOUNCE, IN TIME AND EFFORT.
— CLEAR DIAGONAL PATHWAYS MADE WITH BODY, HANDS AND FEET.
— PALM OF HAND LEADS MOVEMENT.

(Practise Parts 1 and 2).

WEARING YOUR NEW CLOTHES:

Outside the snow is gently twirling, swirling and fluttering. Stand still, blow the snow away from your hands. Blow gently and let your hands flutter gently to the floor. Blow, travel and swirl yourself to the floor. Be still.

Let a new part of your body lead you in another direction as you swirl, twirl and flutter to the floor.

Snowflakes drift together and pile up against a door. They lean on the windows, they hang from the eaves. Practise twirling, swirling, fluttering and drifting, moving in all directions. Remember to be still before you're blown away. **(NEW CLOTHES, PART 3).**

With your new clothes you are snug and warm, proud and happy. Join with a friend and practise dancing the same sequence. **(Repeat NEW CLOTHES, PART 3).**

See photograph.

LOOK FOR:
— DIFFERENT BODY PARTS LEADING; HANDS, FINGERS, ELBOWS.
— STILLNESS.
— A TURNING GESTURE.
— USE OF LEVELS; HIGH, MEDIUM, LOW.
— SLOW, SUSTAINED GENTLENESS.
— A CERTAIN PROUDNESS ABOUT THE SEQUENCE.
— PARTNER RELATIONSHIP.

(Link all three sections, cutting the cloth, putting on your new clothes, then twirling and dancing.) **(NEW CLOTHES, ALL PARTS).**

45

patterns

Patterns, Part 3: Children move in line behind a leader, as if marching downstairs.

STIMULUS:	*Patterns in a wallpaper book.*
DISCUSSION AND OBSERVATION:	Choose a favourite design. Talk about the pattern, shapes and colours. Do any repeat? Look around the classroom. What designs can be seen? What is a pattern made of: lines, shapes and pictures.
LANGUAGES:	Creative writing: • Read the story of Louis Braille (Ginn 360, *Signs, Symbols and Codes*). Children retell in own words. Write in Braille. (Use paper punch to make holes). Make Braille stories. • Write an adventure for Dot (see 'Warm-up' section) • Write in shape poetry. (see 'Calligrams', in *What's in a Poem*, Bill Boyle, Collins). Write rhyming patterns.
SCIENCE:	Investigate fingerprints. Find out about Morse code; sound patterns; radio waves; light waves.

Make observational studies of patterns in nature: tree, leafprints, tree bark, annual rings, fruit designs (especially if halved).

Look at man-made patterns: architecture – arches, brick patterns, chimneys.

MATHS:
Sequences: put out shapes or numbers. Ask children to continue the pattern.

Tessellations; tiling; rotational symmetry.

Number patterns: on separate '100 squares', colour in the answers to the Times Tables.

BOOKS:
The Patchwork Cat, William Mayne, Puffin.
The Owl Service, Alan Garner, Armada Lions.
Lettercraft, Tony Hart, Heinemann.

POEMS:
Patchwork Quilt and other poems, selected by Joan E. Cass Longman.

MUSIC:
'Patterns', Moriel Gidney, *Time to Dance* tape, Belair Publications Ltd.

ART AND CRAFT:
Needlecraft. Children sew a sampler with variety of stitches: running, cross-stitch, herringbone, zig-zag. Create own designs after planning on paper first.

Collage: make up collage pictures from observational drawings.

Use pasta shapes to make repeating designs, or fill in an outline.

Develop pictures from the patterns made by: lines on a road map, brick patterns, everyday objects: oven (spiral elements, rectangular grill pan, handles).

Paper sculpture: fold squares of paper, make cuts at regular intervals, then raise each section. Display against a contrasting backing paper. (Could be used to decorate gift cards. See illustration)

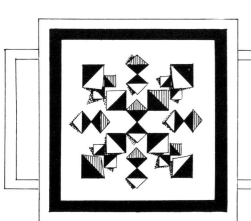

WARM-UP:

(First tell this story. Then repeat it so the children can move to the words.)

"Dot was very small and wanted to grow long and straight like Line down the road. By stretching in all directions and standing tall and straight, or lying out long and straight, Dot became a line. She decided to visit friends, so she travelled. As she travelled she noticed she left a trail. She began to plan: first she turned a corner, then another, and another. She stopped and turned a sharp right angle. 'What fun', she shouted, 'I can turn round and round, on the spot or travelling along. Even better, look, I can make a circle.

"A spiral came next. She began to scribble a jittery shakey line all around. However, this made her very tired. She began to get slower and slower, until she lay down and shrank back to being Dot."

———————————— • ————————————

CURVED PATHWAYS:

Do you remember the names of some of the shapes and patterns that we have been looking at?

Draw a curved line on the floor. Trace a curved pathway across the floor. Stand with one arm curved in front of you, as if you're holding a bundle. Allow the arm to lead you on a curved pathway. Slow down and stop. Take a quiet breath as you change arms. Off you go in another curved pathway.

Try this with the music. Listen for the pattern of music phrases **(PATTERNS, PART 1).**

In your own space can you use any part of your body to trace a curved pathway; on the floor, in the air, around your body. Imagine you are a wave, or a snake. Lead with the back of your hand, and your head. Practise with the music, using four different curved movements. **(Repeat PATTERNS, PART 1).**

LOOK FOR:
– CURVED PATHWAYS.
– FOREARM LEADING, SMOOTH CHANGE OF DIRECTION.
– QUALITY OF CURVED MOTIF: WHERE IT REACHES, HOW IT IS DRAWN. CHECK THAT HEAD AND BODY ARE IN GOOD POSTURE.

(The children could be encouraged to finish the sequence by forming a large circle).

48

ZIG-ZAG:

Listen to the music first **(PATTERNS, PART 2).**
Stand up, point one elbow towards a corner. Allow your elbow to lead you. Stop, change elbows, allowing this elbow to jab the air. Run again. When you repeat this with the music you will see you are tracing a zig-zag pattern.
Stay in the space you have arrived at. Jab your elbows into every space. Practise a sequence of jabs so each time you perform it is the same. Repeat this sequence of events (run and jab, stand and jab). Practise with the music. **(Repeat PATTERNS, PART 2).**

LOOK FOR:
– QUALITY OF FIRM, ANGULAR MOVEMENTS.
– DELIBERATE CHANGE OF DIRECTIONS.
– DIRECT PATHWAYS.

(Children could be encouraged to come together in lines by the finish).

DASHES:

In lines of six (pairs for infants) practise marching about the hall. Try to keep together. Practise trotting. Try to be one unit, not individuals, so that you dance as a line. Try with the music. **(PATTERNS, PART 3).**
The descant notes are the 'stair motif' notes. The leader begins to march downstairs, by bending his knees, keeping back up straight. The group perform this in unison: 8 steps down, 8 steps up. Try with the music. **(Repeat, PATTERNS, Part 3).**
(When the children have assimilated and performed this to your satisfaction, give them specific pathways to follow, perhaps ending in a square formation: line next to line).

See photograph.

LOOK FOR:
– QUALITY OF TEAM WORK.
– CHOICE OF STEP PATTERN.
– OVERALL FLOOR PATTERN.

Link all three sections together: the curved pathway, the zig-zag, and the dashes. **(PATTERNS, ALL PARTS).**

satellites

Satellites, Part 2: Partners hold hands and one turns under the arched arms, while the other circles around.

STIMULUS:	*A picture of our Moon.*
DISCUSSION AND OBSERVATION:	Explain the definition of a satellite: a heavenly body, a follower, a companion, a space vehicle; that the Moon is a satellite of the Earth, and that the Earth is a satellite of the Sun. Look at a chart of the Solar System. Explore the idea of one object circling in a set pathway, i.e. an orbit.
LANGUAGE:	Creative writing: Stories written by a satellite on its orbit: careful detailed discussion and preparation work needed. Analogies of a satellite — a moth around a flame; dolphins around a ship; fairground rides; baby elephant around its mother. Recite and discuss poetry from *Spaceways: An Anthology of Space Poems,* Oxford University Press.
SCIENCE:	Satellite communications: telephone, television, weather forecasts. Discuss the moon and its effect on tides. Read extract from *Charlie and the Chocolate Factory,* Roald Dahl, Puffin (chapter on the transmission of the T.V. Kid).
MULTI-CULTURAL:	Find out about the Moon and its importance in the astrological calendar. Study the calendars of various cultures. The Moon Festival — a Chinese celebration. (*Festivals and Celebrations,* Katherine Elliot, Young Library).

P.E.: To explain satellite transmission, and develop sending and receiving skills: bounce balls from one surface to another.
Use hoop targets at various distances on the floor; thrower takes up central position and throws to moving fielders.

BOOKS: 'Many Moons' from *Stories for 8 Year Olds,* ed. by S. and S. Corrin, Faber and Faber.
Hamlyn Encyclopedia of Space, Ian Ridpath, Hamlyn Publishing.

POEMS: 'Moon section', from *Wheel Around the School,* Macdonald.
'Hi Satellite', from *One Potato, Two Potato, Action Poetry,* Macmillan.
'Moon Poetry', from *I Like that Stuff,* Oxford University Press.
'Soft Landings', Howard Sargeant, from *Once Upon A Rhyme,* ed. by S. and S. Corrin, Faber and Faber.
'Spaceman's Complaint', Barbara Ireson, from *Rhyme Time 2,* Beaver Books.

MUSIC: 'Satellites', Moriel Gidney, *Time to Dance* tape, Belair Publications Ltd.
'The Planet Suite', Holst.
Space Themes: BBC Radiophonic.
'Carousel', from Musical games for children of all ages, E. Nelson, pub. Stirling and Co.
'War of the Worlds', Jeff Wayne's Musical Versions.
'Theme from the Cosmos', Vangelis.

ART AND CRAFT: Pictures illustrating analogies (see Language section).

Moon and Earth pictures made by printing on a laminated table-top: outline large circle in black paint, fill with blue, white and green paint. Swirl with hands. This is the Earth. (Same procedure for Moon, using small circle, with grey, yellow and white paint). Print on paper, cut out and double mount on black.

Junk models: Collect plastic yogurt display trays from supermarket. Carefully cut up into interesting pairs of shapes. Paperclip front to back, and then decorate with metal objects, and suspend. (Items used in illustration include paperclips, shower hook, snap fasteners and drink can pulls). Satellites can be completed by drawing astronaut onto sticky label. (See illustration)

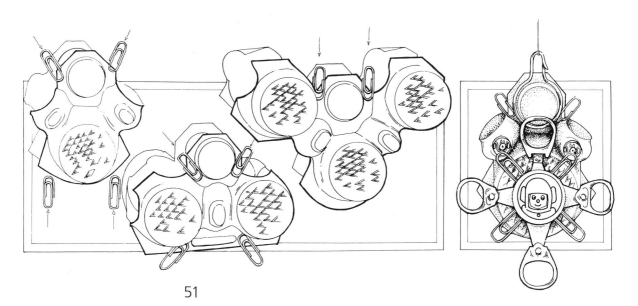

WARM-UP: Lead all the children by the hand into a large descending spiral and out again. Walk, trot or skip.

———————————— • ————————————

SATELLITES PART 1:   The stars are studded across the sky. Make sure you are in a space of your own and take up a rounded position on the floor from which you can move easily. Slowly rotate your whole body as if you were on a display turntable.
Reach out an arm and draw a large circle, as if you were describing a water wheel. Use your foot, head and any other part to describe a large, slow-moving wheel. Stretch and reach to make the wheel large.
Slowly begin to stand up, turning as you move. Try this several times with the music. **(SATELLITES, PART 1).**
Try to turn as an ice-skater turns; cross one foot over the other, closely at the ankles. As you take the weight on the crossed foot, bend both knees and use all the body weight to turn you completely, thereby uncrossing the feet. Stretch as you rise.
Join these two sequences with the music. **(Repeat SATELLITES, PART 1).**

LOOK FOR:
– QUALITY OF STILLNESS FOLLOWED BY SUSTAINMENT AND SMOOTHNESS. (THIS IS THE ESSENCE OF THE WHOLE DANCE).
– EXTENSION OF GESTURE.
– AN UNDERSTANDING OF CIRCLE PATTERNS – A WATER WHEEL OR STIRRING A MIXTURE.
– ABILITY TO TRANSFER WEIGHT CAREFULLY.

SATELLITES PART 2:
(Partner work)   Now spin away, spreading low and wide, keeping the arms wide to describe a large orbit. Spin towards a partner.
Listen for the change in the music, then circle each other. One stands still as the other circles the opposite way. Now pass back to back, taking large fluid steps to end up at the starting position.
Join right hands to make a high arch. One partner turns continuously under the arched arms, while the supporter walks in a circle. (This makes a circle within a circle). Practise the whole travelling sequence with the music. **(SATELLITES, PART 2).**

See photograph.

LOOK FOR:
– TRAVELLING GESTURE.
– PARTNERSHIP, WORKING TOGETHER AND IN OPPOSITION.
– UNDERSTANDING OF THE PATTERN OF THE DANCE.

(Practise Parts 1 and 2.)

SATELLITES PART 3:
(Partner work)

Spin across to a third partner. Stand with your feet in the centre, hold hands and lean outwards, so the weight is balanced and the effort shared. Step around the central spot, remembering to move slowly and smoothly.
Break away and find other ways to circle each other. Change levels, change speed, change direction.
Finally, repeat the opening section of Part 1: Cross step and turn, moving down to the floor, circle body parts and finish in stillness. Try this with the music. **(SATELLITES, PART 3).**

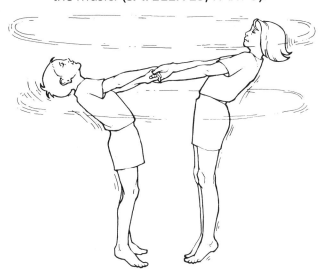

LOOK FOR:
– QUALITY AND CONTROL OF SPIN
– WEIGHT SHARING (HAVING A CENTRAL POINT AND A LOW CENTRE OF GRAVITY HELPS THE SPIN).
– USE OF LEVELS, SPEED, AND EFFORT, TO CREATE INTERESTING VISUAL DYNAMICS.

Link all three sections. **(SATELLITES, ALL PARTS).**

statues

Statues, Part 3: The statues come to life and rock 'n' roll together.

STIMULUS: *Read the extract from 'The Lion, the Witch and the Wardrobe', where Aslan frees the creatures of Narnia from the White Witch's spell.*

DISCUSSION AND OBSERVATION: What are statues normally made from, and why do you think these particular materials are used?
What stories could a statue tell? (a statue from Buckingham Palace Gardens, or from a museum.)

LANGUAGE: Creative writing:
- Stories told by a statue.
- A conversation held between a visiting pigeon and a garden statue.
- 'The statue that came to life'.
- Exploration of names introducing capital letters and abbreviations (e.g. V.C., R.I.P., O.B.E.)

HISTORY: Stories of the lives and legends behind famous statues:
- Nelson's Column in Trafalgar Square.
- Eros in Piccadilly.
- The Statue of Liberty.
- Statues in your neighbourhood.

MULTI-CULTURAL:	The Hindu world and its statues of Gods and Goddesses (from *Religions of the World* Series, Macdonald Educ.).
P.E.:	Balance and stillness: activities such as travel, freeze and hold. Repeat with apparatus. Weight-taking activities; weight transference. Games such as Dead Lions, Statues, or Camouflage (children fake or mould themselves into the shape of the apparatus: good for shape exploration).
BOOKS:	*The Luck of Troy*, R. L. Green, Puffin Books. 'The Envious Athlete', from *101 School Assembly Stories*, Frank Carr, W. Foulsham & Co. Ltd. *The Lion, the Witch and the Wardrobe*, C. S. Lewis, Fontana.
POEMS:	'The Statue', Edith Roseveare, from *Message, a Book of Poems*, compiled by N. Lewis, Faber and Faber.
MUSIC:	'Statues' Moriel Gidney, *Time to Dance* tape, Belair Publications Ltd. 'The Sorcerer's Apprentice', Dukas.
ART AND CRAFT:	Statues made from pegs: wool wrapped around to make trousers and top. Add hat and accessories. Wire sculpture: mould clay, plasticine or paper mache around wire. Make individual or class statue. Still life drawing of a real statue. Design an unusual water fountain. For older children: drawing on stones, using black and white pencils. Dark felt tip (permanent all surface marker) combined with white pencil very effective. Fix afterwards with spray fixative. A book on early sculpture would be a useful reference. (See illustration)

WARM-UP:
Sit on the floor with legs slightly apart. Slide one foot back towards your body, raising the knee, and then slide the foot away along the floor as if pushing sand. Repeat with the other leg. Push, push, push. Now rest against your hands, bend your legs, feet off the ground, and bring your toes down to tap, tap, tap. Push the hands into the air as if pushing away the clouds, push, push, push. Finally the hands reach out to tap the air, tap, tap, tap.

STATUES COME TO LIFE:
You are statues, standing still and forlorn. You were captured and, in mid-action, frozen solid.
As the music starts, allow one body part to pulsate with the music. When the music phrase changes, introduce a head movement, and finally a foot action. Raise and lower the foot in time with the music. Practise with the music. **(STATUES, PART 1).**
Now the statue has been released, the dust has to be shaken off. Shake one hand, then the other (changing with the music phrase). Brush one arm, and then the other. Pretend to swing a hat around above your head. Repeat with the other hand. (This is called hand-jiving). Practise and repeat the series of movements to the music. **(Repeat STATUES, PART 1).**

LOOK FOR:
— STILLNESS. THE ENERGY IS HELD WITHIN THE CENTRE OF THE BODY AND NOT SEEN AS TENSION IN THE BODY.
— UNDERSTANDING AND FEEL FOR THE MUSIC: A BOUNCE AND SWING STYLE.
— PULSATING GESTURES SHOULD BE FIRM AND DIRECT.
— STRETCHING THROUGH BODY PARTS.

DANCING STATUES:
Now you are free. Skip in all directions, making sure your change of direction is clear. Skip forwards, skip in a small circle, skip the other way. As you repeat this pattern, join up with one other dancing statue. With your partner, skip forward, break and skip in a circle; skip in the other direction; rejoin and skip onwards. Come to rest at the end of the music. Face your partner. **(STATUES, PART 2).**

56

LOOK FOR:
– HAPPY, BOUNCY SKIP.
– USE OF MUSIC PHRASES.
– DIRECT AND CIRCULAR PATHWAYS.
– CONTRAST BETWEEN STILLNESS OF FIRST SECTION, AND THE TRAVELLING OF THIS SECTION.

ROCK 'N' ROLL:

Listen to the next part of the music. **(STATUES, PART 3).**
Stand facing your partner. Shake right hands, shake left hands. Repeat with each hand, changing when the music changes. Join both hands. Swing arms from side to side, four times.
Swing arms to one side, but swing them high so the lifted hands make an arch. Turn under the arch and complete one full circle. Circle back the other way. (You will need to keep your hands held loosely so they can swivel. You should have rolled under and around.)
Practise this sequence with the music. **(Repeat STATUES, PART 3).**
Can you now make you own rock 'n' roll sequence? Use some of the steps I've taught you. You may like to try some of these:
1. Hop, step and kick.
2. Walk around partner, back to back.
3. One partner turning under arch, followed by the other.
4. Hand jiving.
Practise with the music. Link your sequences and mine together to form a Rock and Roll dance from the beginning. **(Repeat STATUES, PART 3).**

See photograph.

LOOK FOR:
– CO-OPERATION BETWEEN PARTNERS.
– OPPORTUNITIES FOR STEPS TO BE PERFORMED WITH A BOUNCE.
– DYNAMICS: KEEP A COMMON ELEMENT IN THE ROCK 'N' ROLL.

(Link all three sections, looking for overall contrast between the still, pulsating opening, the travelling, and the rock and roll). **(STATUES, ALL PARTS).**

time

Time, Part 1 (dressed for a special assembly): The Grandfather clock sways and plods: a great contrast to the cuckoo clock and the digital clock.

STIMULUS: *A collection of clocks.*

DISCUSSION/ OBSERVATION: What is a clock? Compare the clocks on display. Do they look, sound and work in the same way? What moves?
What other time pieces have you seen?

LANGUAGE: Creative writing:
- Early memories
- 'Out of the future'
- Time travel (read an extract from Nicholas Fisk's *Time Trap*, Macmillan Educational)
- Why did the mouse run up the clock?
  Where did the mouse go?

Time sayings: Just in time; Time, gentlemen, please; Time's a great healer.

Vocabulary:
adverbs: before, after, during, meanwhile, still, slowly.

Story beginnings: Once upon a time, long ago.

SCIENCE: Seed growing activities: record time and stages of growth.

Making clocks: sand, water, and sundials.

Study of pendulums.

The ageing process: body changes from baby to adult.

MATHS:	Reading the time. Estimating and measuring time. 24-hour clock. Time, distance, speed equations. The calendar.

HISTORY:	Historical time: a comparison of then and now.
	e.g. dinosaurs/forest — horses/woodland
	       caves — bungalows
	       sailing ships — QE2

MULTI-CULTURAL:	Special times and festivals depending on the month when the topic is undertaken. Birthday, Anniversary, Funeral: many are acknowledged in different ways in different cultures. Look at several contrasting cultures.
BOOKS:	*Bedknobs and Broomsticks,* Mary Norton, Puffin Books. *Tom's Midnight Garden,* Philippa Pearce, Puffin Books. *Children of Green Knowe,* L. M. Boston, Penguin. *Stig of the Dump,* Clive King, Penguin. *The Ghost of Thomas Kempe,* Penelope Lively, Puffin.
POEMS:	'I used to have a little red alarm clock', Michael Rosen, from *Rhyme Time 2,* Beaver Books.
MUSIC:	'Time', Moriel Gidney, *Time to Dance* tape, Belair Publications Ltd. 'My Grandather's Clock', Henry Work, *Appuskidu,* A. & C. Black. 'Song of the Clock', Leon Rosselson, *Tinder-box,* A. & C. Black. 'Cuckoo Waltz', Moussorgsky.
ART AND CRAFT:	Record the passing of time; half trees in spring, the other half in winter. Display pictures of the class as babies and at present, and paint portraits of what they think they'll look like in ten years' time. Observe the workings of a clock, its cogs and wheels. Make a collection of broken clocks; use the oddments to make pictures. Print pictures of clocks: soak a flat sponge with thick paint in a shallow dish. Press everyday objects onto sponge pad and print with them. Items used in illustration include lids, rims, handles, screws, child's bricks, pencil and ruler ends, pencil sharpeners, cotton reels, curtain hooks and paper clips.

WARM-UP:

Sit down. How can you tick like a clock, using only your legs? Find another way. Try using only your back. Try another way.
Stand up. Gallop this way and that way, trying to make very tiny steps. Rest. When you change direction, stop, breathe, and then continue. Use different shaped pathways.
Finally, stand with your feet apart, punch the air all around you, straighten your arms to the tips of your fingers. Sit.
Let's repeat the whole warm-up. Imagine you're the inside of a clock, ticking happily, then you're the cogs travelling around. Suddenly the springs break and you break.

———————————— • ————————————

THE GRANDFATHER CLOCK:

The grandfather clock is the oldest and slowest of all clocks in the land. Sit down and listen to the music of the grandfather clock. **(TIME, PART 1).**
Without the music, let's try walking like a grandfather. First, he sways from side to side, and then he tries to walk forward, stepping diagonally and sinking into deep bends. He plods forwards, backwards and around in a circle and begins swaying again. Let's try this with the music and repeat the whole pattern until the end of the music. **(Repeat TIME, PART 1).**

See photograph.

LOOK FOR:
– A WELL-BALANCED STANCE.
– USE OF BENDS.
– UPRIGHT BODY POSITION: THE HEAD CARRIES THE BODY FORWARD.
– DYNAMICS: USE OF ARMS (OPPOSITE ARM PUSHES DOWN IN THE DIRECTION OF FORWARD-STEPPING FOOT).
– FLUIDITY OF SEQUENCE.

THE CUCKOO CLOCK:

Sit down and listen to the music. Can you hear the occasional cuckoo call? **(TIME, PART 2).**
The cuckoo clock is much more energetic. It calls out whenever it can. Use a high-stepping jogging action: jog forwards, backwards and around in a circle. When the cuckoo calls out, step forward, leading with your chest, throwing your hands and arms, outstretched, behind you. Try this with the music. **(Repeat TIME, PART 2).**

60

LOOK FOR:
– CONTROLLED JOG,
SHOULDERS DOWN AND
BACK STRAIGHT, KNEES
HIGH, LIGHT STEPPING.
– GOOD USE OF CHANGE
OF DIRECTION.

DIGITAL CLOCK:

Sit down and listen to Part 3. **(TIME, PART 3).**
The numbers on a digital clock change subtly, fading from one to another. Practise moving through your own space in a series of shapes and gestures: each should be stretched and held. In this way you should make a shape, take a breath and pause, make a gesture, take a breath and pause, and so on, for the length of the music.
You may like to try this with a partner.

LOOK FOR:
– DISTINCT CHANGE OF
SHAPES BY DIRECT
MOVEMENTS.
– SUSTAINED QUALITY OF
MOVEMENTS.
– ORIGINALITY.
– IF PARTNER WORK
UNDERTAKEN, SAFE USE
OF WEIGHT SHARING.

Link all three sections with the music. **(TIME, ALL PARTS).**

weather

Weather, Part 3: Children leap the puddles while the thunder crashes.

STIMULUS: *A selection of postcards showing scenes of weather conditions.*

DISCUSSION AND OBSERVATION: 'Weather is lovely. Wish you were here' — traditional greeting. Why mention the weather? Why is it so important?
Discuss the children's experiences of weather.
Observe variety of pictures to do with weather: Renoir's 'Les Parapluies', Monet's 'Wild Poppies', and other Impressionist works.

LANGUAGE: Creative writing:
- 'Caught in a thunderstorm'.
- 'The long hot summer'.

Vocabulary linked with weather conditions: rain, wind, snow, hail.

Listen to and map gale warnings in Shipping Areas.

Weather proverbs: explain, discuss, illustrate, e.g. storm in a teacup, make hay while the sun shines.

Sort a variety of equipment and clothing for specific weathers.

SCIENCE: Study weather: water cycle, precipitation, cloud formations, Beaufort Scale and wind.
Weather forecasting and monitoring: related experiments.
Weather extremes and the geographical prospect: desert, mountain, rain forests etc.
Adaptation of animals and plants to specific weather conditions: hibernation, migration, growth of thick coat, nocturnal animals; plants of varying leaf types.

62

MATHS:	Recording, measuring and estimating of temperature, rainfall, sunshine etc., depicted on graphs.
MULTI-CULTURAL:	St. Swithin's Day (15th July) Noah's Ark – the Flood Australian Aboriginal stories of *How the Earth Became, Stories and Rhymes*, B.B.C.
BOOKS:	*Bringing the Rain to Kapiti Plain*, V. Aardema and B. Vidal, Macmillan. *The Weather*, Frances Wilson, Macdonald & Co Ltd. *The Rain-God's Daughter and other African Fairy Tales*, retold by Annabel Williams-Ellis, Blackie.
POEMS:	'Getting up Early on a Spring Morning', Po Chü-i, from *A Flock of Words*, collected by David Mackay, The Bodley Head. 'The Rainy Day', Rabindranath Tagore, from *A Flock of Words*. 'Go Out', Eileen Mathias, from *Fancy Free*, Poems selected by D. Saunders, Evans Bros. Ltd. 'A hot day', A. S. J. Tessimond, from *Time's delights*, chosen by R. Wilson, Hamlyn.
SONGS AND MUSIC:	'The Weather', Moriel Gidney, *Time to Dance* tape, Belair Publications Ltd. 'Weather Song', *Tinder-box*, A. & C. Black. 'The Wind Blows East', *Appuskidu*, A. & C. Black. 'Oh, What a Beautiful Morning', *Boomps-a-Daisy*, A. & C. Black. 'Snowflakes are Dancing', Debussy. 'L'Apres de Midi d'un Faun', Debussy. Sound Effects, BBC Radiophonic Department. 'The Four Seasons', Vivaldi. 'Sing a Rainbow', Arthur Hamilton, *Appuskidu*, A. & C. Black.
ART AND CRAFT:	Make a weather vane. Paint weather pictures from music and story stimulus. Draw pictures to match proverbs in language section. Mobiles: Children draw pictures of themselves in either summer or winter clothes, and make an umbrella or parasol with cloud/sun or cloud/lightning as shown. Both sides of figure and cloud should be decorated and then the assembled figures suspended as shown, with their umbrellas. (See illustration)

WARM-UP: Pretend to hop from one paving slab to another and finally leap the puddles. Find your way through fog and mist in a forest. Carefully step under, slide around, and leap over the trunks. As the fog lifts and you find yourself in a glade lie down and sleep.

———————————— • ————————————

SUMMER SUN: The warm weather has arrived. It makes you feel lazy and sleepy, like a cat basking in the sun. Lie in a space on the floor, and allow your body to stretch.

Lie face down on your tummy. Place your hands, palms down and turned inwards, under your collar bone. Push your head and chest away, the hands taking the body weight. Lift one leg high, stretch it across the back of the other. Allow this leg to pull you around until you are sitting up. Continue the roll but take the weight on one arm and one leg and relax onto your tummy.

Try this again, but draw a large circle with your arms as they are freed, then gracefully roll back onto the floor, tummy down. Fill the music with rolls, first in one direction, and then the other.

Really try to make a lazy, stretched roll. **(WEATHER, PART 1).**

LOOK FOR:
– FEELING OF LAZINESS.
– STRETCHED LIMBS INCLUDING POINTED TOES.
– CONTROLLED ROLL.
– USE OF BREATH TO HELP INITIATE THE PULL UP.

AUTUMN WIND: Just as a piece of paper caught by the wind will be lifted up and sent spiralling away, so you're inflated and scattered, spiralling faster and faster.

Start by sitting on the floor, with legs outstretched and one hand resting on the floor behind you (just close enough to the small of the back to be comfortable). Begin to roll over, but as you stretch onto one hand and foot, draw a spiralling line in the air, making it reach higher and higher. Push your body up so that the whole body is outstretched between the supporting hand and foot. Feel like a helicopter taking off.

Now, relax the body onto the floor, quickly roll over onto the knees and stand up. At all times the arms and hands should be extended and tracing a wide spiral pattern.

Continue to spiral on the spot, dipping low and rising high, then break out into a spiralling shape that grows wider. Make changes of direction to avoid dizziness. Travel in all directions. Try with the music. (WEATHER, PART 2).

LOOK FOR:
– OUTSTRETCHED LIMBS.
– SPIRAL PATHWAYS WHICH START SMALL AND GRADUALLY WIDEN.
– GESTURE OF HAND THAT LEADS THE SPIRAL.
– CONTROLLED SPIRALLING.

(Link Summer Sun with Autumn Wind)

THUNDER:

When it is going to thunder the air becomes heavy. The rain pitter patters down until the thunder crashes, then it rains heavily and each drop is very powerful.

The wind left you spiralling. Continue to do this, but pause with the music and flick your hands away from the body. Imagine they are very wet. Spiral one way and then the other, then leap across the room as if jumping wide puddles. At first make it light and bouncy, but gradually make the flicks and leaps heavy and powerful. Clench fists, straighten arms and point toes.

As a group, practise leaping in same direction, to look like the 'wind-driven rain'. Try with the music. (WEATHER, PART 3).

See photograph.

LOOK FOR:
– CONTRAST BETWEEN: SPIRAL PATHWAY AND DIRECT PATHWAY: LIGHT AND HEAVY MOVEMENT: TRAVEL MOMENTUM WITH STILLNESS.
– USE OF GESTURE, WET HANDS, CLENCHED FISTS.
– INTERPRETATION OF THE MUSIC.

Link all three sections, with the music, the summer sun, the autumn wind, and the thunder. Practise the changes from one section to the next, making them fluid. (WEATHER, ALL PARTS).

variations on each dance

Balloons
1. Sequence with group as balloons, together with a new sequence developed for a balloon seller (solo).
2. Group or class activity: children dance sequence but develop dynamics of different times, speeds and directions to make an interesting dance.

Christmas   Christmas messages in different languages.

Clowns
1. Performers dressed as Charlie Chaplin-type figures.
2. Class performance: develop sequences for other circus performers.

Dragons
1. The children creep into a museum and bring a dinosaur skeleton back to life.
2. Group dragon: Individuals dance the opening sequence, and then groups work on idea for group dragon dance. Use umbrellas to hold up a dragon costume: large sheets stitched together in a tube. The leader wears a dragon mask.

Feeling Angry
1. One group are farmers, another are the frightened people, and a third are the pieces of broken machinery.
2. Class develop a series of sequences to fit other emotions, and perform as a kaleidoscope of images.
3. The Row: partners use sequence to develop a row between themselves.

Fireworks
1. 'The Box' (similar to Pandora's Box). Inquisitive children open a box, drop in a match. Fireworks explode.
2. A dance by pets, children and old folk who do not like fireworks.

Flight
1. Flight of birds: develop the quality of sustained movements, work in 'V' formation to represent geese flying and migrating.
2. A prisoner escaping: group develops a following/contrasting sequence. 'The escape, chase, capture'.
3. Child or children represent kite flying in the wind. 'The launch, flight, reeling in'.

Hornpipe
1. Children perform hornpipe as a class activity, perhaps after they have sung a sea shanty.
2. 'Pressganged': One group are pressganged, marched up and made to dance. A second group are the pressgang, who perform alternative movements to the music, at the same time.

Light (Divali)
1. 'Lights': Individuals carry their own type of light, having worked out their own sequence.
2. Fire: group starts in centre of stage area – sequence represents
   fire starting,
   flames travelling,
   fire destroying,
   (Individuals could be clothed in various fire colours).

New Clothes
1. The fashion show: the first and second part are the same. Change the third explanation to the swirling and whirling of the fashion model. The drifting becomes the pose.
2. Perform dance with individuals or partners, using lengths of material to highlight body lines.

Patterns	1. Same dance, but children begin motif from a corner, moving diagonally.
	2. Trios: Curve – carrying stick with streamer.
	            Zig-zag – hands covered with gloves.
	            Line – hat with arrow stuck through.

Satellites	Moths around a candlelight: have one figure as the light, and the rest as moths.
Statues	Children are shop dummies, first frozen in position, and then slowly coming to life.
Time	'Time flies': the first section represents infancy: learning to walk. The second section represents middle years: the hustle and bustle of work. The third section represents later years: the slowing down of life.
Weather	Umbrella dance: group lie on floor with umbrellas resting as sunshades for the first section. For wind section: children pick up umbrellas and use them to emphasise the spiralling wind. Umbrellas should be held close: dramatic gestures suggest rain.

teacher's notes

teacher's notes

teacher's notes

For sales and distribution outside America:

Folens Publishers, Albert House, Apex Business Centre,

Boscombe Road, Dunstable, Beds., LU5 4RL, England

For details of further Belair publications,
please write to:

BELAIR PUBLICATIONS LTD.,
P.O. Box 12,
TWICKENHAM
TW1 2QL,
England.

BELAIR PUBLICATIONS USA

116 Corporation Way

Venice, Florida 34292